LOOK AT
EYES, EARS
AND **NOSES**

Franklin Watts
96 Leonard Street
London EC2 4RH

Franklin Watts Inc.
387 Park Avenue South
New York
N.Y. 10016

Franklin Watts Australia
14 Mars Road
Lane Cove
N.S.W. 2066

UK ISBN: 0 86313 983 3

Editor: Ruth Thomson
Design: K and Co.
Design concept: David Bennett
Consultant: Julian Hector
Illustrations: Simon Roulstone
Phototypeset by Lineage, Watford
Printed in Italy
by G. Canale & C. S.p.A., Turin

Picture credits:
Biophotos 18a, 27
Bruce Coleman 10a, 15b, 22, 23a, 25, 26, 28b
Chris Fairclough 4a, 4b, 4c
NHPA 12b, 16, 18b, 28a
Oxford Scientific Films 10b, 11a, 11b, 24, 29
Zefa 5, 6, 7a, 7b, 7c, 8a, 8b, 8c, 9, 12a, 13a, 13b,
    14, 15a, 17a, 17b, 19, 20a, 20b, 21d, 21b

Front Cover: Heather Angel

LOOK AT
EYES, EARS
AND NOSES

Rachel Wright

FRANKLIN WATTS

London • New York • Sydney • Toronto

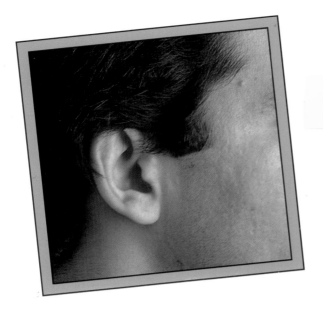

These are our sense organs. They vary only slightly in shape and position from person to person.

We listen with our ears.

We see with our eyes.

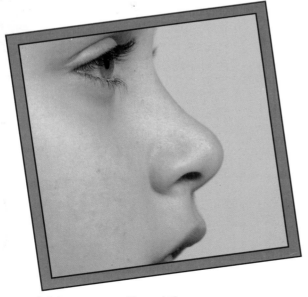

We smell with our noses.

4

Many animals have keener senses than ours.
Their sense organs have developed to suit how and where they live.

Owls hunt at night.
Their large eyes can see in dim light.
Their ears can hear the faintest rustle.

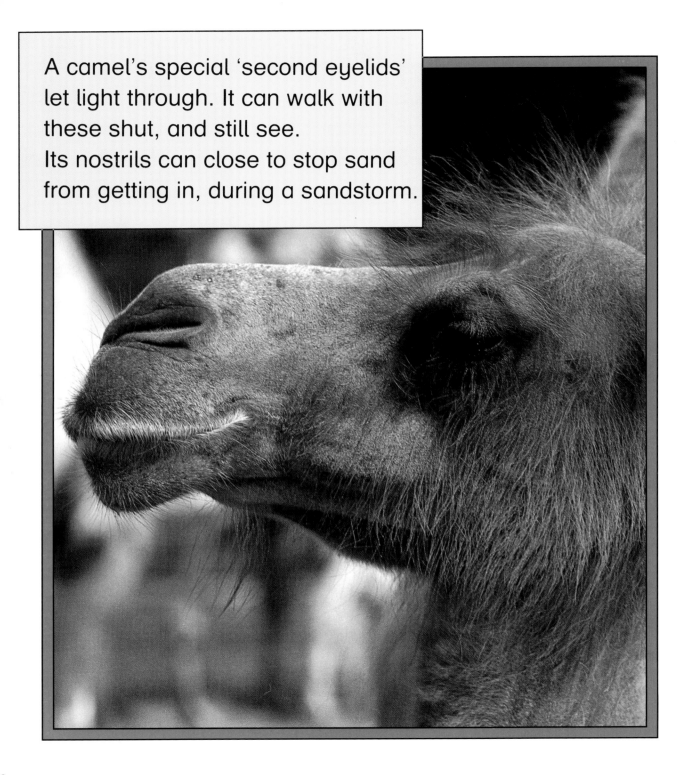

A camel's special 'second eyelids' let light through. It can walk with these shut, and still see.
Its nostrils can close to stop sand from getting in, during a sandstorm.

Ears

Dog

Goats

Donkeys

Mammals have the best hearing of all animals.
They can hear higher sounds than we can.
Most have ear flaps which pick up sound
and focus it into their ear holes.

Often mammals can move their ears
backwards and forwards.
They can work out where a sound
is coming from, without moving
their body and drawing attention
to themselves.

Hares

Pig

Rabbits

Bats that hunt at night are almost blind, but they have keen hearing instead. They find their way by making sounds and listening to the echoes that bounce back to them.

Sound travels a long way
in empty areas like deserts.
Desert animals have
keen hearing.
They come out at night
when it is cool.
In the dark,
their survival relies
on their good hearing.

Kangaroo Rat

Canvas back

Caique

Birds have good hearing too, but they do not have ear flaps. Instead, they have ear holes, hidden by feathers.

Insects have ears
on different parts
of their bodies.
Some grasshoppers have ears
on their first pair of legs.

Spiders have 'ears' on the last
joint but one of all of their legs.

Fennec fox

Desert hare

Large ears and a keen sense of hearing have other uses, especially in hot countries.

These mammals can listen for prey and keep cool by losing heat through their large ears.

An elephant flaps its large ears to keep cool.
It will also spread them out wide
when threatened, to make it look bigger.
This frightens away intruders.

Eyes

Animals do not see the world
exactly as we do.
Their eyes are not always set
in the same position as ours.

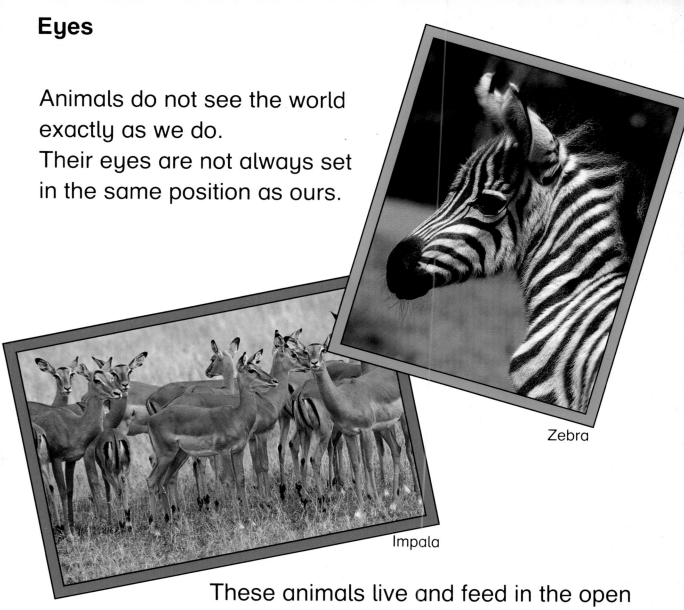

Zebra

Impala

These animals live and feed in the open
There is nowhere to hide.
Their eyes are on the side of their head,
so they can see in front, to the side
and behind without moving.

Many hunting animals have forward facing eyes.
This helps them to judge distance properly.
Their ears often face forwards too.
This helps them to focus their hearing
on the same area as their eyes.

Lioness

Most mammals cannot see bright colours.
They can see only pale shades or grey.
Their eyes are made to spot movement.

Cow

Ponies

Birds of prey have eyes
which face forwards.
A special part of their eye
works like binoculars.
They can spot a small animal
on the ground
twenty metres below.

Buzzard

King vulture

18

Most adult insects have eyes
made up of a lot of tiny lenses.
Their eyes stick out from their heads
so they can see above, behind and below.
Their sight is very fuzzy.

Fly

Crab

Snail

Crabs and snails have eyes on long stalks.
Their eyes cannot see in detail,
but they can recognise light and dark.
This helps them find cover easily
and to know whether it is day or night.

These animals spend a lot of time in water.
Their eyes are set high on their heads.
They can hide their bodies under water
and still see what is going on around them.

Hippopotamus

Crocodile

Underground and cave animals
spend their lives in darkness.
They do not need to see.
Fish like this cave dweller
have no eyes at all.

Noses

Most land animals can smell
better than we do.
These animals rely
on their noses
when searching for food.

Boar

Brown bear

The sloth bear eats termites.
It closes its nostrils as it pushes
its head into a termites' nest.
Then it blows away the dust
and sucks up the termites.

Many animals with a good sense of smell
mark their territories with special scents.
A male rhinoceros urinates around the edges
of his chosen patch.
Other rhinos recognise the smell and do not enter.

Most animals use scent to attract a mate.
Female moths smell different
when they are ready to breed.
The male picks up the female's smell
with his antennae and follows it to find her.

Fish have well developed noses.
Salmon lay eggs only
where they themselves were born.
They use their sense of smell
to find their way back
to their birthplace.

Some animals' noses
have other uses
as well as smelling.

The Malayan tapir uses its nose
as an extra finger to pull food
nearer to its mouth.

This monkey's nose acts like a loudspeaker.
Its warning honk can be heard
some distance away.

Do you know?

● Animals with large noses do not necessarily have the best sense of smell. Eels have nearly 100,000 tiny sense detectors and can smell almost as well as a tracker dog.

● The elephant is said to have a sense of smell as good as a moth.

● A squid found in New Zealand has the largest known eyes in the animal world. Its eyes were 40 cm across. Squid have good eyesight, but probably see in less detail than humans.

● The scallop has more eyes than any other creature. One scallop may have between 50 and 200 eyes around the edge of its mantle. The eyes can detect both movement and the difference between light and shade.

● The only mammals that don't have ear flaps are dolphins and toothed whales.

Things to do

● To which animals do these ears belong? Look through the book to find the answers if you can't remember.

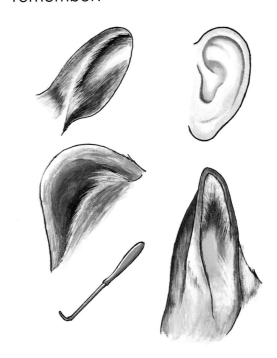

● Test your own field of vision. Hold a pencil straight out in front of you with your right hand. Keep your head facing forwards and don't move it. With your arm extended, move the pencil slowly to the right. Notice how far round it goes before you lose sight of it.

Now do the same thing with your left hand. What do you discover about your range of vision? Are your eyes similar to a hunting animal or to those of a hunted animal?

● Look at these two pictures of bats. One is a fruit eating bat, the other is an insect eating bat.Which is which? What are the differences between them?

● When you next visit the zoo, look at the position of different animals' eyes. What clues do their eye positions give you about their living and feeding habits? Keep a notebook in which to record your findings.

Words and sayings

Can you find what these words and sayings mean?
bull's eye
cat's eye
hawk-eyed
eagle-eyed
pig's ear
earwig
donkey's ears
nosey
To see red
To get an eyeful
To make sheep's eyes
Blind as a bat
To bite someone's nose off
To count noses
To be led by the nose

Index